*Hit*Box

*Hit*Box

& other poems

Kara Dorris

© 2023 Kara Dorris. All rights reserved.
This material may not be reproduced in any form, published,
reprinted, recorded, performed, broadcast,
rewritten or redistributed without
the explicit permission of Kara Dorris.
All such actions are strictly prohibited by law.

Cover art by Jason Hawke
Cover design by Shay Culligan

ISBN: 978-1-63980-478-8

Kelsay Books
502 South 1040 East, A-119
American Fork, Utah 84003
Kelsaybooks.com

Acknowledgments

Thank you to the following publications where these poems originally appeared:

8 Poems: "Ladies' Night at Ace Hardware"

a) glimpse) of): "Medusa Swings Perseus's Head Like a Bowling Ball," "To Whoever Linked Symmetry to Beauty," "Why I Might Be an Octopus," "A Noose for Every Occasion," "Because Everything Is Poisoned with Desire"

Conduit: "Shelter in Place"

Defunct Magazine: "Aubade with 20/20 Vision"

DIAGRAM: "The Baby Sloth Syndrome"

Entropy: "Guide to Being Born"

Gigantic Sequins: "Car Wash Ars Poetica"

The Jabberwock Review: "White Light"

Lit Break: "Mirror Neurons," "Unity of Opposites," "Nocturne with Flame," "Ode to Mayo Jars"

Maiden Magazine: "Love Poem as Nyquil Commercial," "Into the Blue," "Odalisque"

Monstering: "Setting the Table," "Ars Poetica with Physical Therapist"

One Art: "Stargazing Where 'Stop' Means 'Yield'"

The Revolution: "Life Story," "Advice to My Twenty-Four-Year-Old Self"

RHINO: "Liget or Lightning"

So to Speak: "Ghazal with Absence & Fruit"

Stone Circle: "*Hit*Box: What Princess Peach Says to Mario After He Rescues Her"

Waxwing: "*Hit*Box Ars Poetica"

Wordgathering: "Beauty's Pulley System"

Yes Poetry: "Anaphora of Impossible Desires"

Contents

absence as reward

Wasp Nest as Pinata	15
Ghazal with One-Sided *Hit*Box	16
Stain-By-Numbers	18
Life Story	19
Let's Say We Didn't, Tragically,	20
*Hit*Box: Gender	21
Shelter in Place	22
*Hit*Box Ars Poetica	23
Ghazal with Pain & Absence	24
*Hit*Box: Damsel in Distress	25
The Madness Vase	26
White Light	28
Stargazing Where *Stop* Means *Yield*	29
Survival Strategy	30
Ode to Mayo Jars	32
Nocturne with Flame	33

blow slowly to ease the sting

Liget or Lightning	37
Anaphora of Impossible Desires	39
Ladies' Night at Ace Hardware	40
*Hit*Box: Game Babe of the Year	41
A Dandelion's Last Act	42
The Baby Sloth Syndrome	44
Ars Poetica with Physical Therapist	45
The Growlery	46
*Hit*Box: Daddy Issues	47
Mirror Neurons	48
Epistle with Gunshot Wounds	50
Mother as Possibility	52
*Hit*Box: The Perfect Woman	53
There Will Be No Celestial Mentions Here	54
Ghazal with Fruit & Absence	55

don't eat your heart out

The Pulley System of Beauty	59
*Hit*Box: Beauty as Symmetry	61
Nights of Desirable Objects	62
*Hit*Box: Love at First Sight	64
Setting the Table	65
Love Poem Disguised as NyQuil Commercial	67
Unity of Opposites	68
*Hit*Box: What Princess Peach Says to Mario After He Rescues Her	69
Ouroboros IRL	70
Because Everything Is Poisoned with Desire	71
*Hit*Box: Champagne-Glass Legs	72
Odalisque in Pieces	73
Why I Might Be an Octopus	75
Asylumville	76
Medusa Swings Perseus's Head Like a Bowling Ball	78
Half-Girl's Survivor Ghazal	79

a guide to being born

Aubade with 20/20 Vision	83
The Mind Is a Furnace Burning the *Almost*	85
Heart to Stone	86
Guide to Being Born	87
*Hit*Box: God Codes	88
A Noose for Every Occasion	89
Aubade Ending as an Accessory	91
The Mouth Can Speak Without Words Until It Can't	92
In the Blue	93
Advice to My Twenty-Four-Year-Old Self	94
*Hit*Box: Dress-Coding	95
CarWash Ars Poetica	96
*Hit*Box: Waiting to Be Rescued	98
Dear Bravery	99

A hitbox is the invisible shape [around the body] used in video games for real-time collision detection.

"Empathy is always perched precariously between gift and invasion."
—Leslie Jamison, *The Empathy Exams*

absence as reward

(not your madonna/whore)

Wasp Nest as Pinata

I thought it was something to hit, as if we were meant
to hit. I thought what fell out would melt
in the mouth, would feel good against tongue
& cheek. I imagined all those wrapper-wings
crumpled under foot & fist. I thought those snaps
were mint chocolate eggs although I know
the sound of breaking bones. I thought we should stop
shaping pinatas as cute nothings: bunnies, donkeys,
shooting stars. As things that never harmed
except by filling these bodies with expectation.
I thought pinatas should be shaped as our demons,
the things that tempt & betray: family, skeletons,
death itself, a wasp nest. The thing that leaves us alone
until we disturb it, the thing that teaches us
to mind our own business. I thought I could splinter
my anxious guts by spilling someone else's, link
nose & tastebud & nails, sweeten the sting. I thought it was
an outlet for rage & rage's grief. Absence as reward.
I thought it wanted to be beat until it opened
& emptied. I thought I was owed something.
That I owed pain. Thought we could wrap pain
& vulnerability & scarcity in Bubblicious bubble gum,
in raspberry milk chocolate, in paper mâché
& streamers, in mystery, in the physicality
of hitting & being hit, & then we could hit until
there was nothing left.

Ghazal with One-Sided *Hit*Box

after the damsel in distress, Lady, who needs to be rescued in Donkey Kong

We didn't even have a name at first. Just *hey lady,*
let me rescue you. From captive to girlfriend, all ladylike

& demure. I had a hitbox & hits were scored—
a ladylike fall down the stairs, a ladylike

slide into a door-jam—but ladies don't hit back
or tiger claw guys   in the nut-sac. *Hey lady*

as a whip snap,   a backhand slap,   an oven.
Hey lady, watch your step. Disinformation, all *hey ladies.*

As if we don't see the danger right
in front of us,   strangers call out on streets *hey, lady*

you've got some dangerous curves. As if our hips are salt
& pepper shakers to spice up   their worlds. *Hey lady,*

that fine red dress should be illegal. I was tragedy, a lounge singer
without voice. Now, I tip my hat low over one unladylike

stink eye. I mean, I wasn't even playable. Just another damsel
in distress   on a construction crane   told to *act like a lady.*

Come on, baby-cakes, let's go for a ride. Just hang around
my neck, tight. I'm at your service, my lady

(as long as you play along). Eventually, they named me.
When I returned four decades later, not-so-ladylike,

I played myself & no other. Not your madonna or whore.
I wanted to be more than a plot point, a reward, a lady-

bug to admire & wheel over & crush. Remember:
you can rescue yourself, Pauline. You are no one's lady.

Stain-By-Numbers

I used to love cartwheels & handstands, diving to
the bottom of a pool to retrieve a diamond ring or lost
scrunchie. Didn't fear being turned upside down
or whirled around. Not the pressure of water pushing
air from lungs. Didn't fear the Underworld fruit;
I was no Persephone, no Hades was going to fall in love
with my tattered one-piece swimsuit. My mother was not
going to kill the world for half a year if I disappeared.
I couldn't tell you what a pomegranate looked like,
too focused on apples. I thought I was only
a female body, not a body of knowledge. I knew
so little. I knew oranges dyed my fingernails
the color of sunrise. I knew wasp nests begged
to be pinatas. I knew my hair was more baby snakes
than tadpoles, more than dead bodily excess.
I knew my Pitbull mix was not Cerberus even though
he bit that one boy who tried to cross my River Styx.
I knew better mediums existed beyond melted crayons
& paint-by-numbers—a stained-glass knife that twists & turns
with each wrist flick, the one that only starts the break
& awaits the right amount of pressure; the soldering iron
& wire mistaken for silver neck extension collar. I was
that girl-body kaleidoscoping. I didn't see the danger
in the light that cut through all her twirling limbs.

Life Story

They said mustaches are illegal if
you habitually kiss people.
That we can't carry ice cream
in our back pockets on Sundays
but can marry at fifteen
with parental consent.
They said women can't cut their own
hair without husbands' permission,
that one-armed piano players
must play for free—
tell me, my friend, who decides?
Who said, *where the crowd is,
there is truth*. Who forgets
he also said, *there is untruth too.*

Who decides a rapist gets
parental rights?
Who said stillbirth is concealment
& crime? We must fear
our bodies & walking at night.
In a catholic hospital they say *do
no harm* includes forcing "proper burial"
after miscarriage, choosing between
mass grave or private
at our own cost, doubling-down
loss when forced to write *mother*
as "relationship to remains."

So, tell me, who decides what's right?
That question, my friend, is
a puncture of terror,
&, sometimes, I am guilty
of closing my eyes, replacing
one dark with different kind.

Let's Say We Didn't, Tragically,

cut through the ivory peonies
        to the paved street,
throw up or snort out tequila between

        the 5th & 6th floors of the Hilton
drink sunrises to be touched, wake
        beneath monsters then drive

for ice cream, dissolve inevitability
        with our mouths, fail to invent
halo rules on the field, be relieved—

        I'm pregnant, I miscarried—lay down
& take it, pretend to want
        when we wanted nothing but

the clear weight of water minus
        the weight of ourselves, a song
of leviathans & sleep, that mysterious

        Atlantis that is not merely a release
from suffering, but from resistance,
        nothing but a haunt, the razor

wings on thighs, the wallpaper imprint
        on cheek, angel-hair fractures of
the not-healed-quite-right, because no one

        heals right, not right away, maybe never,
all uninsured, pre-existing conditions,

        little pyro fanatics & bits of ember,
football gear & offensive positions.

*Hit*Box: Gender

We're all helmet-hair, square chins, & brick
hips. The same square-faced bricks

stacked up & yet—Jasmine sports
a tube top with breasts etched into her bricks.

Bare shoulders & creviced cleavage,
sashes & belts. Corseted bricks.

At least Hermione is as boxy as Harry,
feet planted on the same baseplate brick.

But we've laid our cornerstones early, the Barbie
effect as peach-covered bric-a-brac.

We have so many ways for building Lolitas
& Ophelias. We keep piling it on, brick by brick.

Shelter in Place

You can empty a place of light,
one strip of duct tape,
one blink, one blackout curtain at a time.
I once would have bet you light
couldn't be packed, couldn't fill
like salt or memories,
couldn't be stacked on top
of itself. Couldn't be wrung out,

like a swimsuit in a water extractor,
the one with instructions
a little like a how-to guide
for medieval torture: see
a heart pressed down a silo, arms
& legs dangle like straps
or twist ties, air swept out
until moisture is suffocated
from the body.

I have no poker face, only win hands
when I ante up on a blind steal.
I guess I have always practiced that drill,
shelter in place as the sirens wail.
When I said, *I know that trick,*
that riddle asking what fills up
but never weighs down,
you answered, *bet,* as in
you already know how that punch feels.

*Hit*Box Ars Poetica

You must arrive—fast or slow—
& play it slant. Take a stance: spread your arms & legs.
You must move into & out of your white space,
air that stings & waits
to fill—your dancer's invading quickstep,
your enemy's roundhouse kick, your captive's
kiss—this is your hitbox.

Straight arm is one box; bent elbow two;
a body in motion can be two or five
at any given time. You can't see
your own hitbox, but neither can they. In video games,
this is how you learn: *you're dead.* Sometimes,
programmers disable rest defense
so you can't admire what hit deals death.
Words are boxes too, you know, one will kill you—*bitch,
little girl, mediocre, gimp.*

Programmed to score, we love to watch
this hitbox porn. Hit against hit. It's easy to assault
just another box. You think distance is
a sparring pad but a hit is a hit is a hit. Yes, it protects
& it also teaches us to hurt
                      & how to
                               & when.

Ghazal with Pain & Absence

You vow to not impose your will on anything,
to not speak in definites, then say *pain is the spiciest thing*.

Unlike you, when I'm sure I'm only moderately secure, but I know
pain is a sting, a needle. I don't know if it's the spiciest thing

our tongues will ever taste. I always choose sweets,
milk chocolate & mangos over spicy things

that burn & numb like pain, which is rarely sweet
without the bitter. Pain scrapes nerve endings like spicy things,

but pain is also a knife blade, a cut, a wounded thing that needs
to wound. Maybe pain is a chili & heartburn kind of thing.

But for me, pain is a lake, a still & drowning thing. A river,
swift & dizzying. But who can say the spiciest?

Pain has never been proven to exist. At this time
I can't state a definite. Maybe you're right about spicy things.

I know to *spice things up* not only hurts but excites like pain,
& pleasure always seems to sting.

*Hit*Box: Damsel in Distress

Defining characteristics: bedazzled
crown, toad minions, gentle rule.
Stubborn but cute. Gets kidnapped
a lot. Give us a pink-gowned damsel
& let us watch two brothers rescue her.
Know where to hit so it really hurts.

Give her cat-like eyes & make her less
than human. Trap her in a tower,
trap her in the fresco above her own
castle gate. Take her from
a beach during vacation, take her
from her garden or from her bedroom,

take her from herself. Give us
a damsel in distress, all heroes need
a quest. Then takeover her mushroom
kingdom—it takes more than kindness
to rule. Let her kiss her rescuer & bake him
a cake. Be a reward for his good behavior.

The Madness Vase

for Gwendolyn Paradice

In every film with a vase, you imagine it breaking.
To call this body *the madness vase*

is a bit too *elephant in the room* for you.
Knocked up or knocked off, you know

a vase is simply a symbol
of a thing not saved,   something denied
redemption & sacrificed

to air, something French-kissing the floor
despite diving hands & bloody lips,
the *to be broken* welcoming

its destruction. When someone brings flowers
you are expected to own a vase. Not display
the temporary kind, the plastic free with flower
deliveries that no one saves. You wonder

what happens when a vase outshines
its purpose, when purpose outshines everything.

Think we should just use cookie jars,
or soda bottles or plastic sacks like fish
at carnivals, anything that safeguards.

Vases get filled, & your hope is
that what satiates is all green stems & sunlight.

But you know anything meant to be filled
is meant to be flooded & sometimes the riverbanks
of your hands—like currents, light, space—

can't flow back to where they began.
It doesn't mean we stop—stop soaking,
stop holding, stop assembling new.

We deadhead, we superglue, we blow glass
from fire. We add vases to our wedding registries,
place Waterford crystal in entryways,
bless the floor with wax coatings.

We brace for the breaking, we watch for it,
but we don't stop. We know somethings are more
enduring for having been broken.

White Light

Drone pilots call heat signatures
white lights of heaven—divine,
paradise, target—do we want to consume
the knowledge or the life,
snuff out essence without
distinction? Should value be in simply
existing? Black & white lines,
like the carnival rule
that says you must be *this tall*
to ride this ride.
What about that movie
when a man becomes quadriplegic,
finds love, & decides to die anyway?
Is it all or nothing? What if
we are nebulas,
a million galaxies in chains?
Once back, astronauts collapse
from sensory overload
proving we enter this world weightless,
& we adapt, like spacewalkers,
to the weight of things, become carnival
workers securing safety belts,
pulling levers & chains.
We live Ferris wheel moments,
quick downswings & ups, beginning
& ending smack in our faces,
but the middle is suspended—stolen
kisses, clasped hands & fears—
so, so distant,   lightyears.

Stargazing Where *Stop* Means *Yield*

The law is the law, some might say,
a fixed constellation, & yet,
who gazes into the black-out of absolute
& what gazes back? Without witness,
is anything alive? Without witness,
is anyone to blame for rolling through
a four-way stop sign?

By which I mean, who listens
to sagebrush or asphalt, thin yellow lines
beneath our tires, tank top straps
or closed eyelashes, the lies our eyes invent
(all that long-dead light we wish on).
Tell me, my friend, when we interpret
stop as *yield,* who gets harmed?

Is it like calling *shotgun,* touching noses
in *not it,* whoever is first wins?
Yield as a reluctant stop
or a reluctant politeness. Is *stop* only
conditional if unchallenged?
What of the female body drunk
& passed out?

Do stars yield to daylight, wildflowers
to wind force? Does grass yield to our weight?
Our weight to choice?
Don't tell me context is only an excuse.
I won't believe you.

Survival Strategy

Light's return time varies between
      basalt rock & treetops.

                  By which I mean,
      what are we   but the distance we create?

Because of light, we know
          the Maya warred,
    didn't always solve conflict
      with human sacrifice.

We can excavate Templar tunnels,   walk
        a Micronesian city of the dead,   or grieve
    New York City's cemetery belt

              from space.
          From space, a million faces

can see 3D using near infrared.   As near
      to history's ghost as we can get.

If you close your eyes,
          you can see loved ones placing
    baby's breath   & polished rocks,
      cheaters sneaking

mementos.   Is this why
      we instinctively tell our secrets
        in the dark?   By which I mean,

we need light to see beneath
            the canopies,
    to avoid wading through swampy mangroves
& mosquitoes, anacondas & human teeth,

those things that watermark & mimic
          affection.   It goes both ways—

who hears a confession
      & doesn't want to hide a reaction.
             Who confesses—

      to stealing Templar gold,
           spying on gravestones,
                  or flowering affairs—& wants to see

another's reaction. & still, you worry
                  that if you illuminate

the whole ghost story,
      it will flashlight brighter,
    excavate deeper than
                your personal terrain can take.

Ode to Mayo Jars

Who knew we shared so much with mayonnaise besides
the scrape of dull knives, spit, & messy pits—

what if I said, live by your mayo's instructions:
keep cool but do not freeze. Tell me, would you *keep,*

knowing they say need is a four-letter
word. Would you *keep,* knowing they believe need

is kin to shame. Would you *keep,*
knowing shame is a bruising wrist, tightening

& retightening the lid. What if
the London Monster pokes your ass with a hatpin,

if the two wolves inside you are fighting,
if you sleep past your sell-by date?

Lao Tzu said, *when you let go of who you are, you become
who you might be.* Not meant to. Will you *keep,*

knowing they believe fear is kin to freezing,
a vacuum-sealed guardrail. Could you *keep* believing

fail is a four-letter word. Tell me, will you lean
into sharp points or housecoat yourself

in bubble wrap, ping-ponging without cut
around   every   softened   curve

Nocturne with Flame

The night means *dream to wake,* the night means
    stop. It means space heater & Jedi snuggie.

What about the end makes us enter it alone?
    The night means I won't see pawprints,

how one back leg drags snow like an exclamation
    or a blessing. The night

means lavender unicorn hair trailing
    wool socks as I walk. Night means grave

magic. Unable to snip those yarn tails, I offer nothing
    except myself. I know my offering

is nothing new, so many use the night to hide from
    sunlit hours. To bribe. *With only four true emotions,*

how can we burn out for the count so quickly?
    The night means blinds closed tight,

lock in to let go. The night means skin scrubbed clean,
    night means bug zappers & zombie blues.

The night means an unknown slouching towards us,
    the night means *stop.* But that is a lie

that guts my lover as if a wax dissection model.
    The night should mean more than partially alive,

I know, should be more than a partial savior.
    So, Night, tell me how to enter you

as flame not cinder   as more than ash & fume.

blow slowly to ease the sting

(little pyro fanatics/bits of ember)

Liget or Lightning

> *for the anthropologist Renato Rosaldo and his wife, Shelly,*
> *who lived with the Ilongot until she fell off a cliff & died*

I haven't had the urge to behead anything today—
not the ice fingertips on branches, not
the tulip roots nesting. Not the twisted steeple
of an ice cream cone. Not the ambition
disguising itself as restlessness.
I didn't dream of the Salem witch trials
or the guillotine, only my grandmother dropping down
the stairs again & again, & then her fingertips
pressed against aloe's fleshy neck.

The aloe plant takes patience to root, to deadhead,
to cultivate. Hands steepled over a churn,
my grandfather made ice cream from scratch.
Sometimes, we can't find pain relief
in store-bought things, not in the cups of another's
tuliped hands. Not in prepackaged words.

They say *liget* doesn't exist in English.
The closest translation is a high voltage emotion,
being forest-lost with wolves in the distance,
a communal unmooring, no neon exit signs
or north stars, so much boiling steam & mist,
you can't help but hunt & sever
a few heads just to get through it. Is that not

why mobs throw stones. Why pain
is a broken guillotine & grief
the shallow slice, a wound inside a wound.
Why healing is a scabbing over, a walling off
flesh from air. There is no closeness,

only distance in translation. No voltage
between confessions, only flint against flesh,
glowsticks rather than forest fires.

There is no trust in a translation that could mean
kinetic or fertile or forest or rage or grief.
A need to stop being feeling's conduit, to let loose
the lightning that enters the heart & exits
the heel or big toe as you kick a severed head
down the nearest pit. But what am I saying?
It's like trying to describe to a lover your grief
as a color he has never seen.

Some only want to see composed grief,
the pretty kind that doesn't leave war marks
on cheeks. They want to say *sorry for your loss*
& not mean it. I guess this is why it's different:
your whole neighborhood refuses to dust
off their machetes when your lover/mother/
daughter dies unexpectedly. Bring casserole
& pies instead. No one offers to behead
anything anymore, not even the requiems
or the flowers.

Anaphora of Impossible Desires

I wanted something simple, I wanted perfection.

I wanted natural
like the body recognizing itself in another
body of water.

I wanted to feel resurrected.

I wanted the past to fulfill its contract, reconcile
that country song,
the one about good old days & daddies
who never go away. I wanted my father to wander homelessly
in another daughter's brain.

I wanted to gag want, & I did (for a while).

I wanted to reframe,
to believe stars, like objects in rearview mirrors,
might be closer than they appear,
repurpose a wall as a bridge, ghost as
half a memory.

I wanted to be the hip replacements
my loved ones needed, cup
his joint in my palm's shadow, its twin cushion
cradling hers, three gaits synced in empathy.

I wanted to vaporize the spit of angry words in Texas heat,
blow slowing to ease the sting.

I wanted us to heal without feeling another's pain.
I wanted us to feel each other's pain so we could heal.

Ladies' Night at Ace Hardware

It started fast one day—too hot, too cold—
we couldn't thermostat. We wandered
aisles of mechanical things,
inventions of hold & holding in,
wondering at the nature
of control, how the Stoics believed that good
was absence of pain, stasis.

How they must have treated their bodies
like guardrails, braced & ready
for impact. Was it safety measure,
deterrent, or warning? We don't know
anything more natural than a body in pain,
no better teacher than change.
We feel too much to have entered
this world as absence,

after all, we began curled up, practicing crash
positions, hearts cradled by claws & wings
not thrumming outside
our bodies. Even the word *nostalgia*
originates with 17th century mercenaries
meaning *to return home & pain.*

If there is only one day,
taken away at dusk & returned at dawn,
what true threshold can we invent?
So, we look for signs like *Ladies' Night
at the local Ace Hardware,* & wonder how
to accessorize with what is given: split lips
& plumbs, Draino of Want.

*Hit*Box: Game Babe of the Year

Once I had an emotional arc—vengeance / murder / guilt / _____

Then a tabula rasa with a loosely defined personality to imprint on

Once I was fate trapped in a cave-in, a final cut scene

Then brought back to life without explanation

Once I could have been a strong female lead not a virtual blow-up doll

A Dandelion's Last Act

        is to give its bits to the wind—
you've seen those tattoos,   the ones always being breathed

           beyond shoulder or wrist.

        Artists never paint it whole, just hands
& mouths that blow.   Sometimes with luck, puffs turn

           into hot air balloons

        or diamonds or wings. No one sees
the underneath,   the ten-inch roots rising up year after year.
           Some say it's lips & wish,

        some say it's a weed or a flower or
a salad topper. Some say   you can eat the ones in

           your yard as poison

        or to lower your blood pressure.
Most wishes are see-through,   invisible from a distance.

           What is it that allows us to believe

        that we can breathe life into anything?
Sometimes you want   something from nothing. You want

           nothing more than a window

        with a panoramic view   of
anywhere else,   the way we piece together photographs

        of Mars so our dusty ground becomes
alien. Maybe in outer space

we can believe things fall differently.   Forget dandelions

          start as   something else.

      Yellow streamers that pale
& seed   before turning   so delicate you want to rip

        just to feel the nothingness.

      Like lace, those patterns that lie,
that make women   gentled   like little girls & ponies

         & angry for it.

The Baby Sloth Syndrome

A firefly is not a fly,
a prairie dog not a dog, catgut
not from a cat.

Did you know baby sloths mistake
their own arms
for branches? Then fall & die. It is

the saddest thing. By which I mean
I understand that tendency,
to realize too late

what you're reaching for is not
what you thought—
a funny bone not bone, a lead pencil

with no lead,
learning what it is by learning
what it isn't

by which I mean, by the time you realize
a falling star is not a star
it's too late to stop wishing

Ars Poetica with Physical Therapist

A blood moon, a sleepless red ache
& I think *once upon a time,*
this is what poets wrote for: heated den
to snowy porch, un-tread
except by pawprints & lovers.
Yet now I am writing about *sitzfleisch,*
the ability to sit on one's ass
& persevere in tediousness, tap dancing
on teacups, which is not just a metaphor.
When tossed gently, those cups slide
across the floor like a bone-spurred waltz.

Sometimes, I am vined by the sky-blue
ceramic bells my mother collected,
how often the bells ended upside down,
but never cracked or filled, unbroken toes
of pointe shoes. We learned to tape
our toes, tape down the bell ringer tongue
like we tape a knee or shoulder injury.
You've said it before—we induce pain
to ease it.

Our hands touch a dozen others. *Induce*
& ease, my physical therapist says, *face it.*
I imagine lifelines in our palms inking
the ones in our care. If only
everyone would stretch the tight
tendons despite hurt,
condition give & take. Ice & heat.
Ease into full mobility. Instead, we hold
the ache inflamed, tightening tendon
tenderness until shutting down—& out—
is the only reprieve.

The Growlery

I've never named that place I go
when hurt, too multiple—
sometimes mine, sometimes
yours. You say *there's not a name
for everything*. I don't believe you.
We think it, it exists, even if
our words are imprecise tides.

My Medusa morning hair,
was once called *elflocks* as if
the fey invented frizz
& nightmares. What do we not have
words for? The cusp of
forgetting—no, we say *early-onset*.
We can't know what we don't know

without words. What word means
to love & hate simultaneously?
When Medusa turned
that first boy-intruder to stone,
she flushed as he got hard, harder,
stone. In that poem, what did that skipper's

nameless daughter say as he strapped
her to the mast? She had to be
fresh & rosy cheeked. He had to
be arrogant, believing he could meet
a hurricane, wind to face.
Are there words for that moment?
Did she hear church bells or foghorns,
hope or lies? Maybe she thought, *this is
the last time*. Maybe she knew
her words didn't matter.

*Hit*Box: Daddy Issues

Don't say I have daddy issues.
It's just a phrase to downplay
& dismiss female pain,
a feature in Playboy.
Defining characteristics: lethal
eroticism as if *it is just natural
to put a vamp chick in black leather.*
Boys pay more attention
to tits & ass. It's a fact.
See the pattern. You amnesia
my Nazi base infiltration
& how I kept the original devils
dead & scattered. Dismiss
my burn-it-all-down vow as
wishful thinking.

Mirror Neurons

after Toulouse Lautrec's La Toilette

Even though you don't face the painter
he captures your face.
Heraclitus asked, *how can you hide
from what never goes away?*

Tense shoulders, despair of
the haphazardly half-dressed.
Somehow you blend with your dresses,
keeping the hardness of the chairs

separate. When a woman tries
to blend like softness
it's because she has none
of her own or she has to work harder for it.

You forget the steel water bin
that matches your skin,
your knee-high stockings,
bright-black, chronicling memories of

fighting against
cold floors, numb feet, heated cheeks.
I know that pose—something to do with having
a backbone that bends not breaks,

not facing it to face it,
looking away to look straight. You've read
H, you know the truth. Salty
brushstrokes, filtered lens,

to face the intimate, you create distance.
What do we see in you that seared,
melted a ring on the hardwood beneath?
Our mirror neurons fire, won't let you be

                anything other.

Epistle with Gunshot Wounds

You're smiling despite your hands cut off—
       scissored by the photographer,

by my paper-doll palms, our dotted outlines
       restoring unprinted memory.

It shouldn't be recreated as sadness—you
       simply sit surrounded by empty

aluminum folding chairs. You aren't motion-
       less but suspended in restlessness,

oil derrick fingers & jackhammer knees.
       Your tropical dress—a pink & orange

daiquiri or sunset, or maybe just a purple
       & yellow bruising. Bright

flower behind one ear. Your cheekbones shine
       like metal. You're pregnant

with a daughter, but don't know it yet.
       In another photo untaken, you look

down, rub circles on your stomach, instinctively
       protect against the luau fire.

They say the word photograph means
       drawing with light. By which I mean,

we have always been tiny pixels of illumination.
       If it is true, that we photograph to empty

the mind, what were you forgetting? I survey
       for wounds: the open flowers

like gunshots, your brightness against
       a dark theater, every competing glint.

Have you smiled at someone like that since?
       & I finally understand what Barthes meant:

someone else viewing would see just a pretty
       smile when I feel fists,

strike after strike after knife. & although
       a photo is not motionless,

in my defensive hands you are a winged
       specimen fastened with pins,

a developing wound, the edges teased open
       a little more with each viewing.

Mother as Possibility

As surrounded by a quilting circle, ladies
in Crocs drinking ice-tea with peach floaters,
laughing at cute husky videos.

As hands, needles clicking, no sore fingers
testing blood sugar. On an anonymous
message board for abused women, defining

gaslighting. As a museum docent staring
at ancient Egyptian pottery, Isis with her seven
snakes. As a Walmart greeter, directing us

towards the hand sanitizer.
As a church choir. Attending water
aerobics, bouncing with Styrofoam weights,

the water holding her as no one else does.
As a cult member. As a panda-nanny or a sloth
squished in a cuddle. Downward-dogging

at goat yoga. As an octopus amidst a shoal
of squid. As perennials, as magnolias,
as grapes on the vine sweat-drenched in

sunshine. As a child learning to knit, to read,
to seed, to love ourselves. As anything but absence.
As anything but the absence she creates.

*Hit*Box: The Perfect Woman

for Evelyn McHale, 1947

She said, *no one should see me like this,*
so everyone did. Did she
mean it? Empire State is not
a highway overpass
or a bridge above
a churning river. I think,
like in everything else, she was lying
by surviving. Walked away from a fiancé,
smiling. Crossed out that line—*he's better
off without me*—as if she could cut
the guilt he'd feel. As if
she had nothing else to give.
That letter—*tell my father I have too many
of my mother's tendencies*—
means *fuck you, daddy.* He left
a depressive wife, why not a daughter.
It wasn't rash. The train ride,
brushing shoulders of New Yorkers,
the slow elevator up 86 floors.
Took off her coat, hung it on a guardrail
to protect her note. Carefully lined makeup
showed the line walked, the cost
of simply breathing. Then, the fall.
Lost both shoes somewhere between the 65th
& 50th. Never one to go halfway.
What luck, to land face up on the roof
of a limousine, Dickinson's black carriage.
She was young & pretty, twenty-three.
She was getting married. Beauty.
That's all you see.

There Will Be No Celestial Mentions Here

I don't believe summer fruits exist anymore.
The nectarine I just toothed into—tongue & fruit
like meshed codes—can be bought in any winter.
I can breathe in verbena & pomegranates
from my Glade Plugin & scented candles.
Watermelon seeds hit pavement as if
spit from teeth every time it rains.
There are things we can't mention
not because we shouldn't but because we should
& dare too much. I won't talk about
the beams Romeo & Juliet kiss beneath,
that Deathstar lovers confess to. I won't villainize
Medusa or wish on rocks hurtling towards us. I will not
make shapes & stories out of proximity or look up.
We've already licensed & copyrighted light. My Circes
lampshade seems real against
the ceiling & when I want to be cooled
against summer's heat & cleansed, I won't need
water, although my oasis is never far away.
I will not try to grab or keep or give or jump over
things I can't grab or keep or give or jump.
I won't blame Eve for your pain or pleasure
or try to define it. No, I won't talk about doomed
lovers as romantic. It's too much privilege,
our summer-less fruit, our silence.

Ghazal with Fruit & Absence

There are some fruits that never show up in poems.
You see apples, pomegranates, & figs in poems.

The forbidden knowledge of Eve & Persephone is
as familiar as the ocean & moon in poems.

You don't see jackfruit, sunchokes, or cherimoyas,
no cucumbers & sea beans of lust in poems.

Starfruit & bottle gourds, like love, are seasonal.
Kisses occur in the springs & summers of poems.

Lovers barren in winters without each other.
Fruit equals sex & reproduction, or lack of, in poems.

The female body as gateway, as canal, as incubator.
As container to be studied & emptied in poems.

Your favorite still lifes showcase ripe fruits in bowls.
You try to describe how they make you feel in poems.

Your hands want to reach & mouth that color, know
knowledge wastes like fruit if you don't share it in poems.

You write self-portraits with peach & raspberry cheeks,
not squash & kumquat butts. The body not real in poems.

I don't want to be the fruit or the flower, the mother or girl.
What's left? Sometimes, I never show up in poems.

don't eat your heart out

(all need/wolf teeth)

The Pulley System of Beauty

I've looked to sky, at Google's search
return for walking the line.

Why I must sing q
to find z. I've always wanted

to believe in compasses,
strings between here & there,

in play-therapy. In fate as a well-
thought-out outline.

I've imagined the equator as yellow
paint, a looping highway

& a sweaty man divining
a tractor. Round & round he inks

only hitting the same spot yearly,
pulling double duty,

eyes high etching skyline. Talk
about infinite repair, a Sisyphean

joy ride. But I don't know
what x I've solved for

to find this y, what formula—
first,   outside,   inside,   last.

I've wanted to believe in tethers between
everything. Guide ropes

in the artic. Ziplines of safety,
infinity bow ties tightening

& tightening. But the world is not
a halo recharging itself.   There are lines

within the body, a pulley system,
that grant us acceptance

of our off-kilteredness.
But what do I know? I'm tugging

on the lines right now, pulling too hard
with my dominant hand.

*Hit*Box: Beauty as Symmetry

Did you need to feel kingly, assign crowns & ladders?
To write the hypothesis of desire?

Did the angel & demon on your shoulders demand equal rights?
Did you need to explain yourself to your mother?

Did you need to assign the physical more weight than feelings?
Was your love interest a pseudoscientist?

Maybe you just loved numbers.
Did you want to invent an artist's gridlines?

Or write an original love poem?
Did you want to flip Time the bird, shoot Nature a middle finger?

Make a mountain out of a miniscule thing?
Ensure everyone's servitude to disappointment?

Nights of Desirable Objects

My mother always said, *we make the truth we choose to believe.*
Summers, we sunbathed at the lake of new names.
      Cabin-lost & lonely, called it tanning,
           fishing with our bodies.

We would cast & bait with DNA & bone knots
      for love or rainbow trout or flounder,
           for mermaids or the co-conspired lies we believe in.

But I always reeled in box turtles—again & again,
my Blue Foxy Jigs gashed their lips. & I'm convinced
    I only seduced the same turtle, over & over,
        his mouth a bloody pit.

We poured ourselves into those lures—
      Rebel Pop-Rs, KO Wobblers, Zoom Tricks—
        the need of skin, mutually exclusive desires,
              the mirror—

Sometimes we baited the night,
the stretch of darker-than-it-has-a-right-to-be cedar pines,
    dared it feel us up, distinguish tumor from breast.

Some days we buried ourselves to mask our scents.

Some nights we did not agree on what lure to leave out at all—
Grave Digger, Storm Wild-Eye, Swedish Pimple—
    a husband's affair, an *I hate you* moment,
      a cut brake line—

Nail polished the steps, left our panties on the clothesline,
left razor blades like teeth, unwashed & dripping,
                        razor blades plague-built & rust-caked.

We shaved every day, but no one came, so we let our armpits grow
as thick & dark as pines,
        skin soft as the pit inside apricots,
                slept where we fell on the porch in cots.

*Hit*Box: Love at First Sight

for Charlie Chaplin's love interest in City Lights, 1931

You don't get a name. Perhaps, you haven't earned it yet,
you are, after all, still blind. Perhaps you were once a Florence or
a Helen. A nightingale or a Troy. An anatomy of a scene.

Stone wall, crossed legs, pinned curls. Your grace,
from a distance, masked your blindness. It was typical *love
at first sight* bullshit. He brought you flowers & stared, loved

until he got close enough to hit; you, perfectly coifed, all lace
& buttercups. Like a still life, you sat, like a film still,
you clasped your hands tight. & then in the face of your beauty,

he rallies, as all good men do, & sets out to cure you.
But, really, what future could you two have? His mustache
would have creeped you out, one kiss would have revealed

his truth: his devotion was never about you. You were just
one more vase to fill with gravity & dandelion fluff, one more
drunkenly embellished *for the love of a good woman* story.

Setting the Table

The wolves are snarling today, so I set the table slowly.
He says, *you're so beautiful,* but one wolf
won't let me believe, & I won't let the other close enough
to lick the good china. You've heard this myth.

One dark, one light, live inside. Feed one
& it survives. When will we learn

what we starve always becomes claw
& teeth & snarl? When we see our own ribs, we begin
to mash & gnaw. It is easier to believe,
to break (& break into) what is seen.

So, I close my eyes & set the table. He says,
you're beautiful today, but one wolf is sacrificing

the other on the altar of our expectations.
Here is a severed paw, red against turquoise fiestaware.
Here is an eyetooth, ivory parsley. *Here,* one blue eye, one
brown. A carafe to wash it down. When will

we remember the myth says if we feed both wolves right—
generosity & selfishness, humility & pride—

we all win? So, today, I set the table slowly,
soothe hands over smooth wood grain, one fork
for each plate. Leave the chairs pulled back, forgiving.
I know those high school girls called my arms & legs retarded

because, like me, they were afraid of their own bodies.
He says, *you're so beautiful.* Fancy dress & made-up

I might believe, but not make-up free. One wolf says
he only wants sex. One says attraction is beyond bone deep.
Starve one, or guide both—you get to choose.

They say *beauty is symmetry.* I set the table slowly today,
the wolves are snarling.

Love Poem Disguised as NyQuil Commercial

Because he brings honey cough drops
not cherry   buy one
get one half off

     30 bites   night & day
NyQuil   & strawberry Twizzlers

Because he never has to say
     if you give food
     you give your heart too

Because he brings Dairy Queen
chicken strips & ice cream—
     Oreo   not Reece's—
     & a pup cup for our husky

Because we watch two-for-one films—
The Breakfast Club & Die Hard—
     from Family Video

Because he leans in breaking quarantine
risks the coughing waves
swipes away tangles, breathes deeply
without drowning

Because I take & take

We are mercenary in pain
It's never been so apparent—
they say the Dead Sea is dead
because it can receive fresh water
but not give

Unity of Opposites

We've passed a lot of sad gas station slot
        machines. At best, I can say I haven't

stopped to play. I'm afraid if I do, my mirror
        neurons will fire like sparklers,

like rows & rows of dinging sevens
        & cherries. No turning back then,

even as you aim to say, *just once more.* I once
        watched a man hopping an extension ladder,

laughing at each jarred landing & fracture,
        & wanted to try. Ladders with rubber

soles are best, I was told. In below zero
        temperatures I watch my husky digging face

into snow, such joy in his paws but I buddle
        with gloves & hat, scarf-wrapped.

Yes, someone else's is still someone else's,
        & there's no more to say about that.

Except for our willingness to exist halfway,
        to suspend belief of want versus

need, a missing link between
        desire & end result, the thing & the word

that represents, like the worry
        we will be murdered by serial killers when

it's twelve times more likely we will be strangled
        by the lovers sleeping next to us.

*Hit*Box: What Princess Peach Says to Mario After He Rescues Her

I love you like a cruise ship loves icebergs
like the coliseum embraces ruin.
I often like to play the *if-you-were-dead* game
& use your body towel (or the shirt you're wearing)
to dry my hair. I love you like a stamp
on my passport. I use your razor to shave
my underworld areas & secretly watch
& rewind our tv shows so you never know.
I love you like a pair of flipflops loves the tide,
like a split pineapple, like curly hair loves
the rain. Every day I love so many someones
I've never met. They think they love me too.
Yeah, I love you like a candle flame
loves a candle holder. & you, you love me
like a candle holder holds a flame.

Ouroboros IRL

It's bitter & sweet to think we can't always hit what we aim for.

I learned by pulling back, then swinging forward & letting go,
                                                                          eyes closed.

My lover says *you want to keep wrists straight.*

In controlled situations he always preaches aim.

When I swim, I veer one way or another.

In biology labs crickets are anesthetized in cold water, whirled
                                                    like pinwheels against walls.

Orbiting thresholds, we test what turns our stomachs.
                                    What turns us turtle.

Turns us on & upside down.

Once, I made my lover stop the car to save a snapping turtle.

That slow crawl, that hard shell (never stone enough)
                                                      could have been us.

I practice keeping my wrist straight as I let go.

It's bittersweet to think we were aiming for the same thing.

Because Everything Is Poisoned with Desire

We are half of everything here. Half-
mad, half-glad, half-destructive. We never *go all the way,*
as the kids say. We are half-virginal
& half-dominatrixes. Half-filly, half turtle.
That's the way fairy tales work.
No name half-girls.

Experience held above braided heads
like a game of keep away. Girls in fairy tales know
you only get half the story—
action, moment of fall—not the girl
of mud pies, of mac & cheese lace faces.
Four & a half cat lives.

We sum up the *after*. Who knows what path
she takes to that *darkly ever after*. Glass
breaking. So, you hear half
the meaning. But as kids today say,
we don't want to work for it.
So, half we are & half we stay.

She only ate half a peach. Half an apple. Slept
in half a bed. Weaved half a tapestry.
Received half a pony for her birthday.
Curled half-digested in that wolf's stomach lining.
Half a wife, the suspicious, infatuated half.
& he was only half a husband, the half

with a kill plan. So, girls, so sweet, lick, drip,
repeat. The same restless half-gestures, half-beats.
Half an apple bite whispered, *don't eat your heart
out,* but we gulped & gulped, pit & all,
all need & wolf teeth.

*Hit*Box: Champagne-Glass Legs

This is what happens when we are bred
for speed. Only three fillies have ever won
the Kentucky Derby. Only 39 have spiraled its lanes,
electricity sparking the way we charge
our girldom haloes & crowns.

Eight Belles took second place. Did she have to try
eight times as hard to live one life? Was one
not enough, as if she was asking for it,
for the pole-vaulting expectations
of the men in her life.

& still she wasn't worth the nine lives of a cat.
Sired by Unbridled's Song, daughters of
Native Dancers, what else could we girls do
but rumba & run? At the finishing line
her front ankles fractured. & what happens
after? They name a race after her. Wear remembrance
bands. They say, *she just tripped over her feet.*
They say, *horses love to run, get hurt in the pasture*

as much as the track. You see, that barely leaving
the ground, those hooves that skimmed, too far from flying,
is what killed her. Eight Belles ran with, one reporter said,
the heart of a locomotive on champagne-glass legs.

Eight bells signal the end of watch.
Are we *breeding for death?* Girls love ponies
as birthday presents. We share the same fate,
speeding towards breaking or flash freezing in lakes.

Odalisque in Pieces

To calk a leak   choose
        decoupage or   oakum
            a tarred & stripped rope
used to seal cast iron pipes
       & log cabin chinking
             that *off-coming* unraveled
    a thread at a time

we cut up   or out   or into
      We paper-doll   Set
           the drawn & quartered stage
    Then collage   stick & twist
Sail across watery bodies

protect what we can
      the best we can
          while we can
          from submersion
               & submission

& what else is a requiem
      but a way of sticking with
           the dead   or sticking it to
    the dead   or sticking it to
the living since the dead
      in the deadhouse don't feel
         a thing

The dead aren't expected
      to plug anything & yet
         the odalisque is something
   to plug   & is also dead
or she never existed
     A woman in a harem
         is simply parts

of any other woman
       & when a woman is a collage
              of anyone
                     & everyone
                           & no one
    what else is she but dead?

& what else is a decoupaged woman
       but a leaking ship?   A body sailing
            across other bodies
      of water   seasick
with the back & forth
      of another's want

Why I Might Be an Octopus

We eat our arms when bored

Our arms are sucker-covered   with stalagmites & want

We spit paralyzing venom when tasting what we touch

We have blue blood & three hearts

Our neurons are in our triceps & forearms   not our heads

Only some of us have been seen using tools

We use coconut shells like mobile homes & open childproof
                bottles in less than five minutes

We change color in three-tenths of a second

Like to mimic undersea objects & reach into small glasses

Our mouths center our limbs

We are boneless & expulse inky threats

Sex is a death sentence

Males arm with sperm & after birth females live cellular suicide

Some of us prefer to crawl—if we swim too fast, the organ
         delivering blood stops

We siphon, expelling water & breath, live   in abyssal depths

Asylumville

One vacant building is to be expected,
but a dozen red-bricked empties
is haunting, & not just the time-fogged glass

or grass-owned pavements.
There are places you can't explain
if flesh has fled, if the philosophers are right

& *flesh is the pure contingency of presence.*
If our bodies are just empty bowls, just
placeholders like empty words (*just to let you know*)

& empty gestures *(I know, I know)*. Here, place
has retaken presence like a petrifying
well that turns teddy bears

& hands into headstones.
Here is a sidewalk circling a dead tree,
a walkway leading nowhere, a spray-painted door

blocked by metal bench & warning sign:
don't open, dead inside. Benches surrounding
a large stone bolder that screams

punishment. You drove by once
& the benches were empty. Drove by again
& again   & a girl began to appear.

Sartre wrote, *nothingness carries being into
its heart.* What you mean is that you've tested
this, know you can form 15 words from

the letters in *empty*. By which you mean
there are over 54 containing *nothing*.
Beneath all of it tunnels exist.

Tiny ancient caves that haven't seen light
in 5.5 million years & just don't know it yet.
By which you mean what species,

unknown to the rest of the world,
might we house inside ourselves?

Medusa Swings Perseus's Head Like a Bowling Ball

after Luciano Garbati's "Medusa with the Head of Perseus"

The veins in her arms are embossed rivers—they say
she can't be beautiful. They say *monsters*

should be deformed, grotesque, dipping shoulders
& sloping eyelids. They say *a male sculptor can't be the face*

of a feminist movement. Her snake hair doesn't interfere
with eyesight, or with her mouth mouthing *no.*

Over & over. After all, it's a Greek myth
& all the men did it then. Perhaps she sees just another

Poseidon drowning her. She is full of the ocean,
water snakes with its salt. Aligned with sword tip, her right

hand, mind-swing, slings his tears as if
he is nothing, but he hasn't exited this narrative—

if he were stone, he wouldn't be dripping.
An *inversion of the myth* they say—they ask *why nude?*

You ask *why not?* Does it objectify, make her too vulnerable
or too invincible? An artist wanted to reveal the woman

behind the monster, but I don't see a monster at all.
You can't deny loss evolves us.

Half-Girl's Survivor Ghazal

We have this life & no other—it's more than survival
of the fittest, base instinct. To survive

you can embrace it, or you can sleep like flowered wallpaper—
flashdance in the rain or survive

still & open-mouthed, coughing up water.
Pretend to be somewhere else, believe your survival

is someone else's. But you are here & now
& I hear you chanting survival

like that Gloria Gainer song repeating
over & over. I hate that singsong phrase *I will survive—*

although I used it myself last night. I want to strip
away the plastic flowers, freckle & survive

our hate & sunburn. To not depend
on the breath of someone else to survive.

By which I mean, this body is a carnival act.
That funny/tragic kind of surviving

you can't help laugh/cry at, alone in a bathroom stall.
Can we be more than survivalists?

By which I mean, faith's enemy isn't doubt,
but certainty, & I am not certain we will survive it.

a guide to being born

(tap-dancing on teacups)

Aubade with 20/20 Vision

Some mornings all we can hope for is a tumble
of light & color when opening our eyes,
to keep the line tight between *sleep to dream*

& *here & now.* The Ancient Greek *eidos* means
that which is seen. I have always thought
the word came from collision,

to collide & make pattern's sublime babies.
Kaios for *beauty* & *skopeo* for *examine.*
Most mornings I search for signifiers like

the kaleidoscope patent papers: infinite
patterns, granted July 1917.
Would have been worth millions, if not for

thieving optometrists. You would think
those devoted to clearer sight would be beyond
jealousy & greed, would not steal

another's tool for seeing infinity,
for expanding vision beyond 20/20.
Perhaps that's what we should fear: those who steal

sight then replace it, sell back their own version.
& the moral of the story is—our inability
to truly own anything. Oh, I wish I was one

of the egos, the arrogant ones
who believe. That inventor kept inventing:
confetti & glitter, mirror & bone chips swirling,

carousels & power/control wheels
spinning. Who said science and empathy
don't collide? Carl Jung believed to look outside

meant to see in *dreams,* to look inside
meant to *awaken.* Since memory we have folded
mirrors as books, as hands at prayer.

Ignored that pebble underfoot, that sand
caught in unmentionable places,
tiny scratch & itch. Shut eyes against

the dawn through slitted blinds. We chant, *give me
light but not too much, give me knowledge,
but not too fast.* Each morning when I wake,

I find faith in the fact that infinite patterns began
with a single speck
               of trapped cement.

The Mind Is a Furnace Burning the *Almost*

before fleshed, before callouses
on finger & pen
& hammer. Critical hits.

The mind is a furnace burning
cigarette holes in
experience. *Ash,* prophetic
dream. *Ash,* crying jag. *Ash,*
first love. *Ash,* tomorrow you.
Ash, mask.
Ash, real-time strategy.

The mind is a kaleidoscope
of burn & glove, sweat & smear.
Not just a fireplace
or romantic atmosphere, more
than marshmallows & graham crackers,
soda & beer.

The mind is the area of effect
& accountability.
The mind is a furnace melting steel
& glass becoming
sword & crown & spoon
& mirror.

Choose your kindling.
Like a razor across skin, strike
your lighter. Spawn again.

Heart to Stone

When Medusa turned that first man/boy to stone,
she fell ass-over-elflocks,   completely stoned.

You better believe there was a soundtrack—*Hard Rock*
to *Heart-Shaped Box* to *Papa was a Rollin Stone*.

It was the first documented case of munchies; she mouthed
stemmed fireflies, owls on strings, ice-chipped stone.

She thought he wanted it, so proud of his boner.
Didn't he brag about his hardness, his pillar of stone.

He wanted to cement her. To eye & display. A trophy
draped not in gold or crystal or silicone but stone.

Guide to Being Born

When I say plague masks, you imagine *punctures
of terror,* you think *serial killers & torture*

but once those predatory noses
were wards meant to harm nothing

but juniper & mint, bouquets of small deaths
against larger death. Plague doctors

were once taken from the road between cities
for ransom. By which I mean,

there are infinite patterns to hostage the body,
not enough ways to atone. By which

I meant to say, *reframing is the key
to happiness.* Perhaps I'm arguing against myself.

Then again, think of a fetus—experts say
you don't become you without

a genetic stressor. Strange but fitting
that initial spark also encodes our death

& ensures we dread it. By which I meant to ask
what if wisdom, like rain, collects
at our lowest, gasoline for the furnace.

*Hit*Box: God Codes

You have always hoarded cheat(god) codes,
software patches to coerce my words: *do me baby*

one more time or *go balls deep* or *yes, yes, yes, please.*
Butterfly stitch us into Nude Raiders.

So many chivalrous protectors in the virtual world
in need of low psychological investments.

You praise your binocular-view of my breasts
more than my ability to stealth attack & hit.

A Noose for Every Occasion

Our go-to noose
is red, which matches
our glasses & blood
when iron hits air.
Bright pink is Barbie-
pretty but we can't
pull off ending
all our sentences with
exclamations & glitter.
We don't believe
we can be anything.
80 careers in one lifetime
seems too extreme.
Gray is shade, too light
& airy to keep wind
out. One noose is
covered with our words,
suicide note although
poetry can never
be an ending.
That Parisian street
vendor said nooses
come in every color,
so we bought sunset
& cream too. Black
seemed too final, like
tempting fate & we
thought we could resist
the finality of it.
& of course, we can
buy our given mode
of strangulation at a local
Target or Cracker Barrel:

light with pink irises
or indigo with suede dots
& ruffles. The eyelet lace
is masterful, & sometimes
we wrap its see-through
innocence around
& around our
very tangible necks.

Aubade Ending as an Accessory

I don't know how to skin a fish. Have never
asked for instructions. Never woken
at dawn to be a patient predator on the other end of a line.
I imagine fish scales as shiny, sequined dresses,
as mermaid tails, as costumes like our own clothes
& skins that let us masquerade as something else.
Too many Disney movies, I guess. My mother once
said I epically failed as a girl scout. I kept
falling into traps, the one where I personified
everything was my dynamite. As a real as any bear
trap, as any steel jaws wrapped around my ankle.
What if the trees grieved the infant
or aged limbs we burned in our fires? What if
our bodes confused the wind got it lost
from itself? What if the ground was tired of being
bruised by our feet? What if the rocks thrown
into the river really drowned? What about the fish
trapped in nets, trying to get somewhere just out of reach?
How air strangles them as it gives us life
& how the wind must hate knowing it participates
in our mass killings

The Mouth Can Speak Without Words Until It Can't

By which I mean, pandemic masks both stole
& gave us language. I tattoo words
on my body. Who wouldn't live a double life?

By which I mean how do you learn to choose?
My secret life is secret even to itself.
I forget how much the mouth can unmask the eyes.

How much we blame our feelings on the weather.
By which I mean we should blame ourselves,
the rain feels nothing. Everything

boils down our reaction to pain or its absence,
which can be a kind of pleasure. By which I mean,
I've taken a raincheck from personal happiness.

& although I don't understand the metaphor
I remember giving up. By which I mean
I don't work hard enough at forgetting

& self-destruction. There is no shelter in memory,
asylum as horror & involuntary. I have always
taken what people say at face value.

By which I mean, I don't care enough to doubt.
There is a point you can have too much everything,
falling can only last so long. Fireflies are just flies

to swat away during the day, & sometimes you
just have to pretend the falling leaves are falling embers.

I don't know whether or not I could burn down a house.
By which I mean I keep waking each morning.

In the Blue

When a snake loses its skin, *in the blue*
Lose one's scales, lose one's vision

Who can see through transition?
A one-sided conversation, *in the blue*
                               out to sea
                     ghosting

In the blue versus *into*? The *beginning of*
or *in media res*—

or so far gone even distance
                       can't see you

Sheltering-in-place, *in the blue*
A faux fur coat

The split second before a car door closes

Augustine's prayer to *help me be pure*
       but not quite yet

every moment stepping from
                       definition to context

when we know the tune
       so the words don't matter

the long drive home we can't remember

Advice to My Twenty-Four-Year-Old Self

I would say, *you worry about the wrong things—*

falling into routine as if into a salt pit,
rising as quickly as tar

never realize crooked bones don't make you sink
less   or   more.

I would say, *don't worry about the small things—*
be a monster   for a little while longer.

I would want to say,   *debt isn't invisible—*
the aftermath like freckles or swimsuit lines

even if you never left your own head,
you still beach-waltzed the night in the arms
of that army guy.

I would try to show you,   *debt can be invisible—*
     a shelter for homelessness

in secondary trauma locked doors & windows
can't guarantee safety

sometimes giving in feels like gambling.

[. . .] like the Log Run at Six Flags, assembly lines
of prepackaged chips & Barbies, you'll be
the girl never stepping out
of bounds. But you should know,

you can reframe   *make your own*
     velvet rope   *& warning tape*

*Hit*Box: Dress-Coding

My ass loves short-shorts like hikers love poison ivy.
      When coded with camo pants, I break out in rash.

My breasts love that turquoise leotard turned crop-top
      the way a sacred temple wants to be raided.

My chapped thighs love my dual pistol holster like ghosts
      love being mistaken for white sheets on Halloween.

You hate my plait, this electric eel, for the weapon it is
      & how natural it feels.

CarWash Ars Poetica

You have to start *here*, arrive
with no intention
but to be changed. The carwash
always makes me wax poetic—touchless
tunnel of longing, stasis, high-powered
jets. It's not just about cleanliness
or sex. Not hunger, not
preservation or appearances.

Maybe it's the conveyor track, staying
still while moving. The time old tradition of
trying to hold on to *the way it was*
by leaving—that first dance recital, first kiss, first
roped wrist, scraping away sequins,
saliva, burst skin.

Maybe it's purity, water & detergent,
rainbow suds & white noise.
Maybe it's the intimacy of hiding.
Maybe it's the signs: greenlight *go,* red light *no,*
designated escapes—maybe *all this* is what lets us

ride the sheen of brake dust, tire rubber,
& infrared eyes, situate the body:
front wheel push, rear foot pull, aligning us
with empathy's checkered toolbox
or is it a tollbooth?

Inside, you have to ride the wash of awe
when you learn what the world's capable of—
from Tampax-created spacesuits to
the seemingly magical light of fireflies.

Ride the wash of helplessness & shame of an abuse
hotline flyer hung in a woman's restroom,
phone number strips all gone.

You have to hold on & ride, arrive
on the other side despite the hits so hard
even your ancestors hurt.

*Hit*Box: Waiting to Be Rescued

Being stuck in a tower waiting
to be rescued sucks. Like dicks.
Like I'm drowning in FOMO
without release. I'm not supposed to
say dick. Or FOMO. It puts
dangerous ideas in my little feminine
head. But there's only so many doilies
& communion dresses a girl can knit.
& have you ever tried to lounge
in a chaise wearing a ballgown?
Do you know what's under there?
More than cunt & underworld hair.
Braces & spirals & metal to keep
the dress's shape. And keep us
from running away. Or simply running.
& this crown is stupid. It digs
into my head & gives me headaches.
At least they could have trapped me
somewhere that had a library.
When you get here, bring my army
knife, a Glock, & some duct tape,
would you? I'm tired of waiting.

Dear Bravery

I hate the phrase *lady-balls*
by which I mean I missed the stone tablet

defining male testicles as emblems
of strength & bravery;

oh, Bravery, how you are so mis-defined
& misunderstood I hurt for you—

you & I know balls are velvet,
easy bullseyes for knees, the softest

hard targets. We pity those phallic
illusionists; you don't require dragons slayed

& princesses saved; excavating
inner icebergs is infinitely harder

than any erect penis.
When we want to pull ourselves

up by the lacy bootstraps, we yell to
each other: *cunts to the walls, bitches!*

What could take a pounding & keep going
& going? When the time comes

big boys pull up their pants,
but big girls pull up panties, I mean, really,

is there anything female
that hasn't been sexualized already

like my bestie introduced me to the phrase
amazeballs; I wanted to imagine

basketballs, tennis, even badminton, but *balls
will be balls,* as the boys say;

I see rogue waves on the horizon.
I've tried to create an *amaze-cunt* revolution,
but it hasn't taken; *amaze-v* is too easily
mistaken for the word itself

& *amaze-gina* too close to angina, & we want heart
not just heartburn; it takes more

than antacid, it takes cunt, after all,
to go all out & not settle for second.

About the Author

Kara Dorris is the author of *Have Ruin, Will Travel* (2019) and *When the Body is a Guardrail* (2020) from Finishing Line Press. She has also published five chapbooks: *Elective Affinities* (dancing girl press, 2011), *Night Ride Home* (Finishing Line Press, 2012), *Sonnets from Vada's Beauty Parlor & Chainsaw Repair* (dancing girl press, 2018), *Untitled Film Still Museum* (CW Books, 2019), and *Carnival Bound [or, please unwrap me]* (The Cupboard Pamphlet, 2020).

Her poetry has appeared in *Prairie Schooner, DIAGRAM, RHINO, Tinderbox, Tupelo Quarterly, Puerto del Sol, Harpur Palate, Cutbank, Hayden Ferry Review,* and *Crazyhorse,* among others, as well as the anthology *Beauty is a Verb* (Cinco Puntos Press, 2011). Her prose has appeared in *Wordgathering, Waxwing, Breath and Shadow,* and the anthology *The Right Way to be Crippled and Naked* (Cinco Puntos Press, 2016). Recently, she edited the poetry anthology *Writing the Self-Elegy: the Past is Not Disappearing Ink* (SIU Press, 2023). She is an assistant professor of English at Illinois College.

For more information, please visit:
karadorris.com

www.ingramcontent.com/pod-product-compliance
Lightning Source LLC
Chambersburg PA
CBHW030053170426
43197CB00010B/1503